EAT THE FRUIT, PLANT THE SEED

MILLICENT E. SELSAM
AND JEROME WEXLER

William Morrow and Company   New York 1980

Text copyright © 1980 by Millicent E. Selsam
Photographs copyright © 1980 by Jerome Wexler

Printed in the United States of America.
1 2 3 4 5 6 7 8 9 10

Library of Congress Cataloging in Publication Data

Selsam, Millicent Ellis, 1912-
    Eat the fruit, plant the seed.

    Summary: Gives directions for growing plants from the seeds found inside avocados, papayas, citrus fruits, mangos, pomegranates, and kiwis.
    1. Fruit-culture—Juvenile literature. 2. Fruit—Seed—Juvenile literature. 3. Plant propagation—Juvenile literature. [1. Fruit culture. 2. Gardening. 3. Seeds] I. Wexler, Jerome. II. Title.
SB357.2.S44   635'.6   80-13720
ISBN 0-688-22236-6   ISBN 0-688-32236-0 (lib. bdg.)

Acknowledgment for Photographs

State of Florida Department of Commerce, 16
T. Sahara, United States Department of Agriculture,
    Soil Conservation Service, 22
Millicent E. Selsam, 23
Florida Citrus Commission, 29
Florida State News Bureau, 35, bottom

CONTENTS

For Debbie Peterson,
friend, pit-grower enthusiast, and coauthor of
The Don't Throw It, Grow It Book of Houseplants

You can grow stunning plants from the seeds inside the fruit that you eat. When you look at an avocado, think of the beautiful tree you can grow from the pit. The seeds inside grapefruit and oranges grow into small trees with shiny green leaves. The seeds of other fruits such as mangoes, pomegranates, kiwis, and papayas also produce interesting plants. To grow them, you can either buy the fruit or the seeds. Many of the fruits are available in fancy groceries or fruit markets and can be found even in supermarkets. Some of the seeds are listed in seed catalogs and can be ordered by mail.

AVOCADO

Here is the avocado fruit. It looks ready to be eaten.
The soft flesh surrounds the huge seed in the middle.

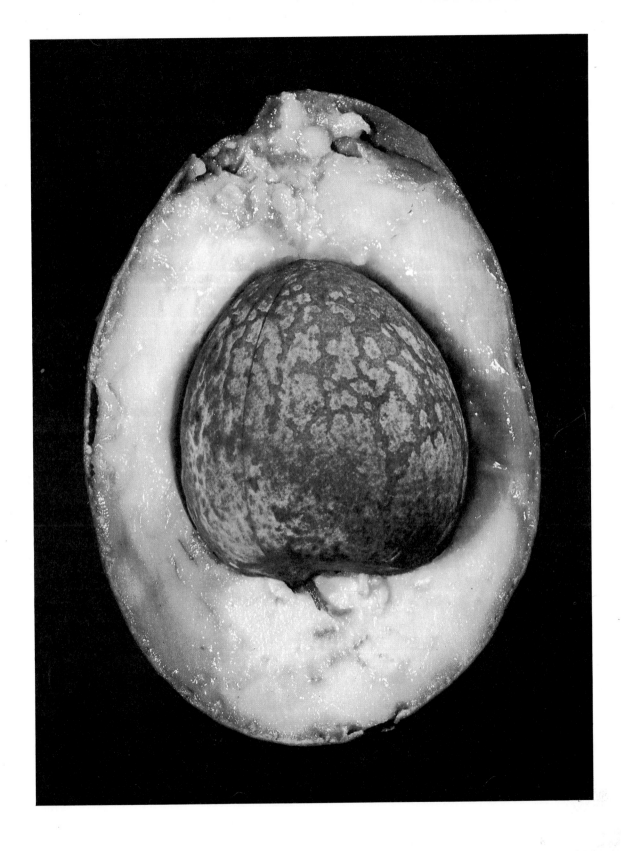

The seed has a brown, papery skin around it. Wash the flesh from the seed in warm water and remove the brown skin. One end of the seed is flatter than the other. This flat end is the bottom of the seed and should always be planted down.

The huge seed may be planted in any one of three ways. The simplest way is to stick three toothpicks around the middle of the seed, spacing them evenly, and place it in a glass of warm water. Be sure the flat

end is down. The toothpicks will support the seed at the top of the glass. There should be enough water in the glass to cover the bottom third of the pit. Then place the glass in a warm, shady place. Keep adding water so that the bottom of the pit is always wet. Change the water, which should be tepid, once a week.

A second way to plant the seed is to put it directly into a pot containing soil. You can buy sterile potting soil at the five-and-ten. Place the seed so that about one half of it is above the surface.

A third way to plant the seed is to put it in a plastic bag containing moist peat. The bag should be folded and put in a warm place. In a few weeks, you will find roots and stems coming out of the seed.

The seed on the left is split in two to show where the embryo is. The embryo is the part of the seed that will grow into leaves, stems, and roots. The rest of the seed is a source of food for the embryo.

Growth will not start for a few weeks, so you must have patience. But suddenly one day the big seed will split and roots will come out of the bottom while a stem works its way up through the middle of the seed.

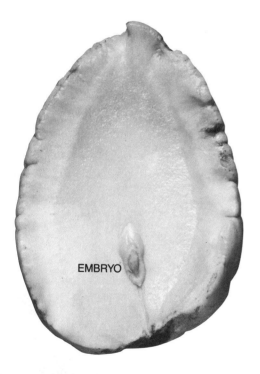

EMBRYO

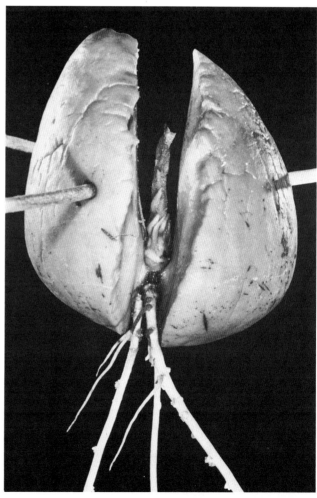

10

If you have used the toothpick method, you must transfer the young plant to a pot. Do so when the roots and stems are a few inches long. Use a pot one inch larger than the seed. Put some soil in the pot, gently place the plant on it, and then fill in soil around it. Leave one half of the seed exposed at the top. Place the pot in a warm, bright place. Avocados will also do well under fluorescent lights.

12

Usually an avocado grows tall without branching. You can let the avocado go its own way until it starts to branch naturally. But some people try to encourage branching by cutting about three inches off the top of the stem when it is around ten inches high.

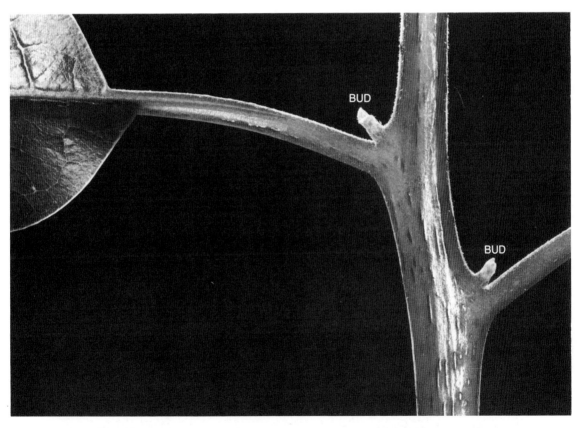

There are buds at the base of the leaves. When the top is cut off, these buds may grow into branches.

This method works very well sometimes as the pictures show. But it is not always successful. You may cut off the top, and then another branch may grow straight up again without the additional branches that you want.

The best idea is to experiment yourself. Plant two avocados of the same kind. Clip off the top of one, and let the other grow naturally.

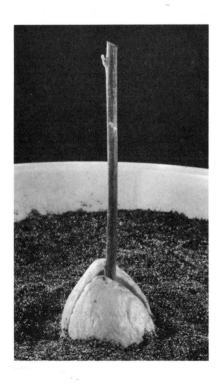

The soil around an avocado must be kept moist but not soggy. When the roots fill the pot and start to come through the holes at the bottom, move the avacado to a pot one size larger. Eventually you will have a beautiful plant like this one.

Outdoors an avocado gets to be
a tall tree and bears fruit.

PAPAYA

The papaya fruit looks like a very large yellow pear.   17

In contrast to the single-seeded avocado fruit,
18   the papaya has hundreds of seeds inside it.

SEED WITH ARIL

WITHOUT ARIL

To plant the seeds, scoop them out of the fruit. The seeds have a jellylike covering (aril). These coverings should be removed by rubbing the seeds on a layer of newspaper. The crinkly brown seed will pop out.

When papaya seeds germinate, they are subject to a fungus infection called "damping off." This infection makes them flop over at ground level. To protect the seedlings, soak the seeds in a fungicide before planting. Follow the directions on the fungicide container.

Plant the seeds in a clay pot. Put broken pot pieces in the bottom of the pot over the hole. Then fill the pot to within an inch of the top with a porous soil mixture through which water flows easily, leaving lots of air spaces. A good mixture is one half perlite (a white gritty material) and one half peat moss. Both perlite and peat moss can be bought at the five-and-ten or at a flower or garden shop.

The clay pot and light soil mixture are necessary because the papaya's roots are sensitive to lack of air.   19

You can plant many papaya seeds in a pot. Cover the seeds with a half inch of soil, and place a plastic bag with air holes over the pot. The bag keeps the air around the pot moist. Then the soil will stay moist for at least two weeks, and you probably will not need to water the pot until the seeds germinate.

The pot must be put in a warm place. Good locations are on a food warmer, on a shelf over a fluorescent fixture, or over a radiator that has been covered by a few layers of newspaper.

The seeds take a few weeks to come up. At this time, move the pot to a bright but *not sunny* place.

When the seedlings are a few inches high, use a pencil or chopstick to lift out the smaller plants. Leave

only the biggest plant, the one that seems to be growing most rapidly. You can plant the smaller seedlings
in separate small pots but do not expect them to be
very successful. These seedlings do not transplant well.

From this point on, keep the pot in a warm, sunny
place and water it regularly to keep the soil moist but
not soaking wet. Use a liquid fertilizer every two
weeks. Be sure to follow the directions on the container. In a few months, your papaya plant will look
like the one in the picture.

Outdoors the papaya can reach a height of twenty to thirty feet. It looks like a tree but technically is not one, because it does not have a woody trunk. The leaves get to look like giant maple leaves. The fruits cluster around the trunk.

CITRUS FRUITS

The most familiar citrus fruits are oranges, grapefruit, lemons, limes, tangerines, and kumquats. Many of them have been bred to be seedless fruits, but actually very few are completely without seeds. Still, if you want to grow citrus plants, ask at the fruit market for varieties with seeds.

Even the "seedless" grapefruit has a few seeds.

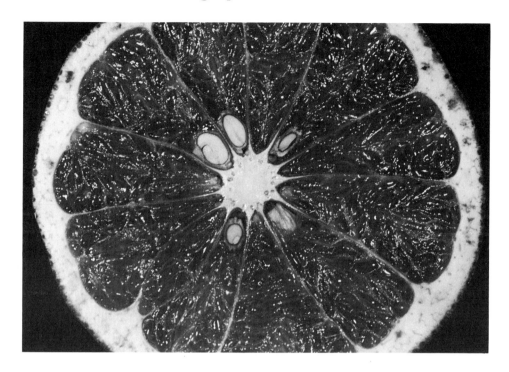

The kumquat has only two seeds.

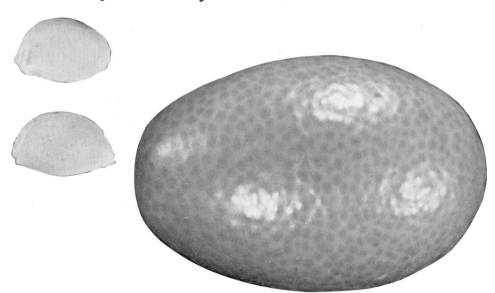

Raising plants from citrus seeds is easy. However, if you have never tried growing any of these seeds before, start with the grapefruit. It is the fastest-growing indoor citrus tree.

Do not allow the seeds of citrus fruits to dry out. Rinse them under the faucet, and plant immediately. Or you can soak them overnight and plant the seeds the next day. Your container can be an ordinary clay or plastic flowerpot, or it can be a plastic dish with holes punched in the bottom.

Mix two parts sterile soil to one part perlite and one part peat moss. Plant a few seeds in each container, and cover them with a half inch of soil. Put the pots in a warm place, and keep the soil moist.

This orange seedling took a few weeks to appear.

Sometimes an orange seed can produce two seedlings at a time.

When the seedlings are a few inches tall, move the pots to a bright but not sunny place. After another few weeks, place the pots where the plants will get at least a few hours of sunlight.

If all the seeds in one pot germinate, you can move the young seedlings to individual four-inch pots. Lift each one out carefully with a pencil or small spoon, and try to keep the soil around the roots as you place the seedling in the new pot. Leave the tallest plant in the original pot. Add a pinch of lime or broken eggshell to each pot.

Citrus plants do well in an airy environment, so if possible keep the plant near an open window or put it outside in the summertime.

This grapefruit plant is about a year old.

Some citrus fruits you may never have heard of are the tangelo, which is a cross between a tangerine and a grapefruit, and the tangor, which is a cross between a tangerine and an orange.

TANGELO

TEMPLE ORANGE,
AN EXAMPLE OF A TANGOR

29

MANGO

The mango is called the "king of tropical fruits" and has been known in India for 4,000 years.

30　The ripe fruit feels soft to the touch.

A very large husk containing a seed takes up a lot of space inside the fruit. The flesh around it is orange and creamy.

After you have eaten the delicious fruit, remove the husk containing the seed. Wash this husk with a stiff brush to remove the pulp that clings to the fibers. Also remove as many fibers as you can.

Most of the fibers have been removed from this husk.

Now allow the husk to dry for a day or two. Then use a nail clip to cut off a piece of the husk. Now get your fingernails inside the husk and pull it apart.

Here the husk is opened. The big seed inside looks like a giant cashew nut.

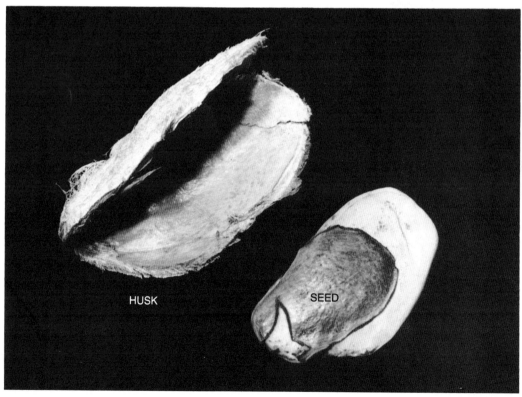

HUSK

SEED

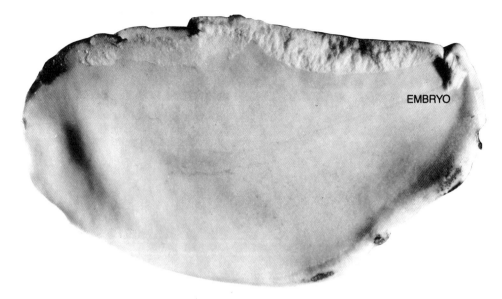

EMBRYO

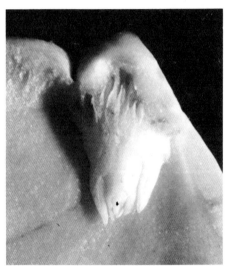

At one end of the seed there is an embryo, which will grow into roots and shoots. The picture on the left is a close-up of the embryo. You can see tiny leaves beginning to form.

Soak the seed for a day. Then plant it horizontally in a pot containing a mixture of half sterile soil and half perlite. Cover the seed with a half inch of soil, and put the pot in a warm place. In two to three weeks, there should be signs of growth.

33

The plant in this photograph is just beginning to emerge from the soil.

A week later the first slim leaves begin to unfurl. They are a shiny, delicate red. Gradually they change to a light green and then to a deep green.

Keep the plant in a warm, bright place *where there are no drafts.*

34

This plant is
ten months old.
In a few years
it will be
a young tree
five feet high.
In the tropics,
grown out of
doors, it bears
fruit and can
reach a height
of fifty to sixty
feet.

POMEGRANATE

Like the mango, the pomegranate was known in ancient times. Today it is considered a delicacy. Look for it in fruit markets in the fall and winter.

It contains many small seeds, each of which is surrounded by a red juicy pulp (aril). You can scoop the seeds out, put them in your mouth, and get a delightful sweet-acid taste.

To grow a pomegranate plant, get the arils off by rolling the seeds on several layers of paper towels or newspaper. Wear an apron because the juice squirts. You can plant the seeds right away or let them dry further until you are ready to plant.

Use a soil mixture consisting of one half sterile soil and one half perlite. Cover the seeds with a quarter inch of soil, and slip a plastic bag over the container. These seeds will germinate in a week or two if you give them bottom heat. You can place your container on a few layers of newspaper on top of a radiator or on a food warmer kept at a low heat level. Without this heat the seeds may not germinate for six weeks.

This picture shows a cross section of the fruit
and the placement of the seeds.

This pomegranate seed has just germinated. When it straightens out, you can see two large seed leaves and the first true leaves in the center.

TRUE LEAF

SEED LEAF

Once they germinate, allow a few plants to grow in the pot and pull out the rest. Several plants grown in one pot will look more pleasing. Also pinch off the top buds of each plant to allow new branches to emerge below.

Put the pot in a warm, brightly lit location. These plants are sensitive to cold, so do not use a windowsill in the wintertime. Keep the soil moist and fertilize every two weeks.

On the right a pot of two-year-old plants shows the bushy effect you can get when several of them are grown together.

KIWI

The kiwi fruit comes from New Zealand, where it is commercially grown. Originally it was found in forests in the Yangtse Valley of China. There it grows as a vine that climbs to thirty feet.

The leathery rind is covered with brown hairs.

A slice through the center reveals its black seeds, lying in the pale green flesh.

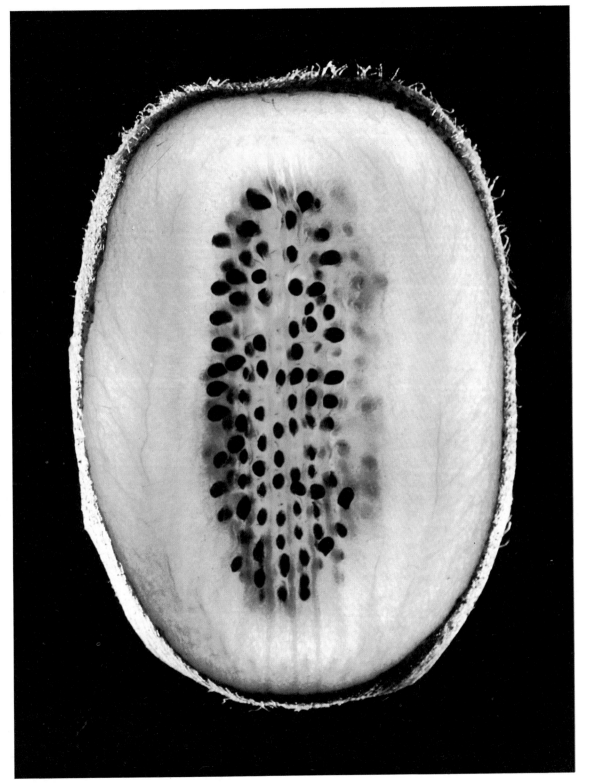

Scoop the seeds out of the fruit, and remove the flesh by washing the seeds in a strainer. If any flesh is left on the seeds after this operation, roll the seeds on paper towels to complete the job.

Put some moist peat moss in a small plastic bag, and mix about a dozen seeds into it. Store the bag in the refrigerator. The kiwi seeds need a moist, cool period to "ripen" so that they can sprout. This treatment is needed by many seeds that fall to the ground in places where winter temperatures are low. The seeds naturally go through a cold, moist period lying on the ground. We imitate this process by putting the seeds in the refrigerator for a period of five to six weeks.

After this ripening period, plant the seeds in pots containing a loose soil mixture such as two parts sterile soil to one part perlite.

When the seeds germinate, they will look like the seedling on the opposite page.

44   The young plant has fuzzy leaves.

SEEDLING

In this photograph you can see that the plant is becoming a vine. At this point, you must give it some support on which to climb.

This kiwi plant
is two years old.
It can be planted
outdoors in places
where the winters
are not too severe.
The top may die
down each year,
but new tops grow
in the spring.

Learn to plant the seeds and fruits described here, and then experiment with others you may find. You will be amazed at the fun you can have, and you will raise a collection of unusual, handsome plants.

WHERE TO FIND THE FRUITS

Most of the fruits can be found in some supermarkets, fruit markets, and in fancy groceries. However, if you live where these fruits never appear, try the following sources:

Alberts & Merkle, Inc.
2210 South Federal Highway
Boynton Beach, Florida 33435
catalogue 50¢

John Brudy's Rare Plant House
P.O. Box 1348
Cocoa Beach, Florida 32931

De Sylva Seed Co.
21994 Tanager Street
Colton, California 92324

J. L. Hudson, Seedsman
P.O. Box 1058
Redwood City, California 94064
catalogue 50¢

Hurov's Tropical Tree Nursery
Box 10387
Honolulu, Oahu, Hawaii 96816

Rare Fruit Council
Museum of Science
3280 S. Miami Ave.
Miami, Florida 33129

Christopher C. Whitman
Whitman Rare Fruit Nursery
23430 S.A. 122 Lane
Princeton, Florida 33032